COYOTE
& THE WINNOWING BIRDS

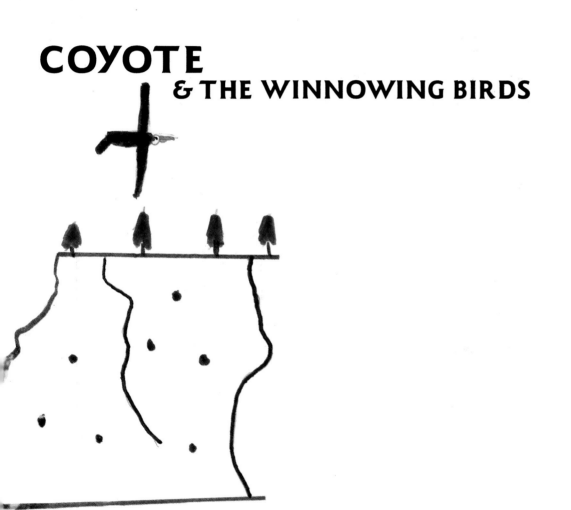

COYOTE
& THE WINNOWING BIRDS

IISAW NIQW TSAAYANTOTAQAM TSIRÒOT

A TRADITIONAL HOPI TALE

BASED ON A STORY
TOLD BY
EUGENE SEKAQUAPTEWA

TRANSLATED
& EDITED BY
**EMORY SEKAQUAPTEWA &
BARBARA PEPPER**

ILLUSTRATED BY
HOPI CHILDREN

CLEAR LIGHT PUBLISHERS
SANTA FE, NEW MEXICO

Clear Light Publishers
823 Don Diego
Santa Fe, New Mexico 87501

Clear Light Publisher's Original Language Series, IPOLA Imprint.
Bilingual Hopi-English edition with glossary.

LIBRARY OF CONGRESS CATALOGING-IN-PUBLICATION DATA

Coyote & the winnowing birds = Iisaw niqw tsaayantotaqam tsiròot : a
    traditional Hopi tale/based on a story told by Eugene Sekaquaptewa;
    translated & edited by Emory Sekaquaptewa & Barbara Pepper :
    illustrated by Hopi children.—1st edition
        p. cm.
    "Bilingual Hopi-English edition with glossary"—T.p. verso.
    Summary: The birds find a way to teach Coyote a lesson when he
tries to trick them. Includes a section introducing the Hopi
language.
    ISBN 0-940666-86-3 : $14.95. — ISBN 0-940666-87-1 (pbk.) : $9.95
    1. Hopi Indians—Folklore. 2. Tales—Arizona. 3. Hopi language—
Texts. [1. Coyote (Legendary character) 2. Hopi Indians—
Folklore. 3. Indians of North America—Folklore. 4. Folklore—
Arizona. 5. Hopi language materials—Bilingual. 6. Hopi language.
7. Children's art.] I. Sekaquaptewa, Eugene. II. Sekaquaptewa,
Emory. III. Pepper, Barbara, 1949– . IV. Title: Coyote and the
winnowing birds. V. Title: Iisaw niqw tsaayantotaqam tsiròot.
E99.H7C69 1994
398.2'097910452974442'089944—dc20—dc20
[[398.2]]   94-12324
                                                           CIP
                                                            AC

The materials in this publication have been developed under a grant sponsored by IPOLA to the Hotevilla-Bacavi Community School. For additional information on IPOLA's educational programs:

IPOLA, The Institute for the Preservation of the Original Languages of the Americas, is a 501 (c) (3) foundation located at 1237 Cerro Gordo, Santa Fe, New Mexico, 87501.

First Edition
10 9 8 7 6 5 4 3 2 1

Printed in Singapore

CLEAR LIGHT PUBLISHERS, in cooperation with the American Forestry Association, has planted trees to replace those used to manufacture these books.

Dedication

When tribal elders pass on, a vast store of knowledge and humanity goes with them. This lesson was brought home to all of us at IPOLA when we lost Eugene Sekaquaptewa. He died not long after telling the story of the Winnowing Birds for this book. He will be remembered as a friend, a scholar,

Askwali!—Thank You!

To the students, staff, library committee, the Board of the Hotevilla-Bacavi School; the storytellers, PTA, and the community of Hotevilla-Bacavi for their patience and support; Le Roy Shingoitewa, Principal, who initiated this pilot project for IPOLA; Leigh Jenkins, Director, Hopi Cultural Preservation Office (IPOLA Board member); Merwin Kooyahoema, the Hopi Tribe video technician, and Michael Bond, Director for the storytelling video complementing this book.

Dr. Carlos Velez-Ibáñez and the Bureau of Applied Research in Anthropology (B.A.R.A.) at the University of Arizona under his supervision, for their guidance and efforts to bring this project to fruition, and for their ongoing dedication and commitment, not only to the Hopi storybooks, but to IPOLA; Emory Sekaquaptewa, B.A.R.A., University of Arizona, for his dedication to preserving the Hopi language with his work on the Hopi Dictionary Project.

Barbara Pepper, translator and editor, for her dedication to this project; Mary Black, B.A.R.A., Hopi Dictionary Project, for her help with editing; Eugene Sekaquaptewa, Field Producer for the Hopi Storybook Project, mentor, and liaison between IPOLA and the community.

Deryck Healy, Alexandra Hess, and Kosta Galanis for their artistic contribution; and Donald Hess for his enthusiasm and continuing support.

Joanna Hess, Founder and President, IPOLA

The Artists

Children of the Hotevilla-Bacavi Community School at Hopi

Cecilia Namingua
(Pongyayesnöm)

Curtis Lomayaktewa
(Tsavatawa)

Marlena Selina

Adam Kyasyousie
(Puhuwayma)

Ariel Paymella

Keith Nutumya

Andrea Salazar
(Pipmana)

Rhonda Lomayaktewa

Gawain Onsae

Duran Howato
(Pisa)

Lloyd Frank

Jerel Quamahongnewa
(Naa'itnaya)

Julian Phillips

Deldrick Poleahla
(Honboya)

Dwight Honyouti
(Hooyawma)

Eric Tenakhongva
(Wuukukiwma)

Eva Bahnimptewa
(Pipletsnöm)

Andree Duwyenie

Alvina Thompson

Tristan Bilagody
(Tokpela)

Gavin Quiyo
(Masakuyva)

Z. Gasda

Winnowing

Winnowing is a way of separating the chaff or outer seed coating from the seed or kernel. Hopis make "winnowing baskets" for this purpose. A Hopi woman will raise the basket quickly, tossing the seeds into the air and catching them in the basket again and again until all the chaff or dust is carried away on the wind.

If there isn't enough wind, she blows across the seeds, like the little birds in the story—*"phhu, phhu, phhu!"*

Yaw Orayve yeesiwa.

Everyone
was living at Oraibi.

Tsiròot taavang Tuuwanasavit
ep piw ki'yyungwa.

There were some Birds also living
toward the southwest at Tuuwanasavi.

Tsiròot sivosit pongitotangwu.

These Birds were usually picking grass seeds.

Pu' Tsiròot pootat aw sivosit ìntotat pu'
put tsaayankyàakyangw tsìipuyat ayo'
pooyantotangwu.

After the Birds put the seeds
in the basket, they would blow away
the chaff as they winnowed it.

Tömö'iwmaqw,
puma a'ni/hin'ur tumala'yyungwa.

Since winter was coming,
they were working hard.

Puma tsaayantotaqe,
puma it tawlalwangwu:

Because they were winnowing,
they were singing this song:

Poota poota poooota,
Poota poota poooota,
    Yowa ini, Yowa ini,
    Phhu, phhu, phhu.

Winnowing, winnowing, winnowing basket;
Winnowing, winnowing, winnowing basket,
    Seeds inside it, seeds inside it,
    Blow, blow away.

Pu' puma puuyàltotikyàakyangw,
töqtotingwu—
Tsii riw riw riw riw riw riw riw!

Then, as they flew up, they shouted,
"Birds birds birds birds birds birds birds!"

Puma pantsatskyaqw,
Iisaw pitu.

While they were winnowing,
Coyote came along.

Pam amumi taytaqe,
pam piw tsöngmokiwta!

He was watching them,
and he was hungry!

27

Pu' Iisaw amumi kwangwawuwanta.

"Sen nu' hin Tsiròotuy ngu'ani,"
Iisaw yan wuuwanta.

Now Coyote was scheming about them.

"Perhaps somehow I could catch these
Birds," was how Coyote was thinking.

Piw Tsiròot
tawlalwakyàakyangw
tumala'yyungwa:

Meanwhile,
the Birds were singing,
and working:

Poota poota poooota,
Poota poota poooota,
    Yowa ini, Yowa ini,
    Phhu, phhu, phhu.

Winnowing, winnowing, winnowing basket;
Winnowing, winnowing, winnowing basket,
    Seeds inside it, seeds inside it,
    Blow, blow away.

Tsiiii . . . riw riw riw riw riw riw riw !

Birds birds birds birds birds birds birds!

Pu' puma Iisawuy tutwa.

Just then, they noticed Coyote.

Sùukyawa Tsiro Iisawuy aw pàngqawu,
"Ya um yep hìntsaknuma, Iisaw?"

One of the Birds spoke to Coyote,
"What are you doing around here?"

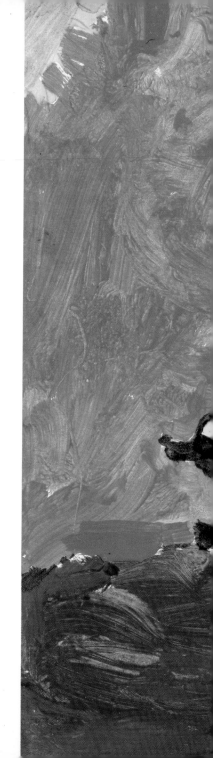

"Nu' as umumum puuyàltini," Iisaw kita, "niikyangw nu' qa masa'yta."

"I would love to fly with you," said Coyote, "but I don't have wings."

41

"Itam ung itàamasay maqayani,
pu' um puuyàltini," Tsiro kita.

"We shall give you some of our own feathers,
and then you will be able to fly,"
the Bird said.

Pu' Tsiròot masay akw Iisawuy yuwsinaya.

So then the Birds dressed up Coyote
with their own feathers.

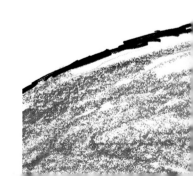

Pu' piw Tsiròot tawlalwakyàakyangw,
puuyàltoti.

Iisaw pàasat amumum oova puuyawma.

Now again while the Birds sang,
they flew up.

This time Coyote was up
in the air flying with them.

Poota poota poooota,
Poota poota poooota,
    Yowa ini, Yowa ini,
    Phhu, phhu, phhu.

Winnowing, winnowing, winnowing basket;
Winnowing, winnowing, winnowing basket,
    Seeds inside it, seeds inside it,
    Blow, blow away.

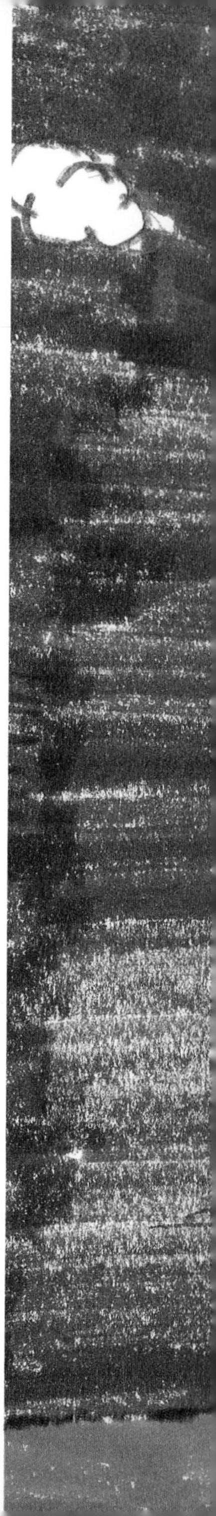

Tsiiii . . . riw riw riw riw riw riw riw !

Birds birds birds birds birds birds birds!

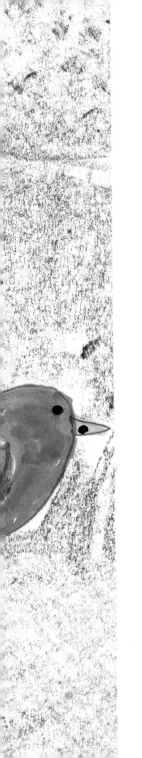

Niikyangw Tsiròot pàasat Iisawuy engem
hin pasìwnaya!

But the Birds had a plan of their own
for Coyote!

Pu' oomiq puuyàltotiqw, sùukyawa Tsiro töqti—Taa!!

Pu' pàasat, Tsiròot Iisawuy angqw masay ahoy tsotspitota.

So now as they flew way up, the one Bird shouted—Now!!

Right then, the Birds snatched back their feathers from Coyote.

Iisaw, okiw—atkyamiq nàmtötötima,
posto, postokyangw, *yeeva!*

Poor Coyote—he began tumbling
toward the ground, down, down, *smack!*

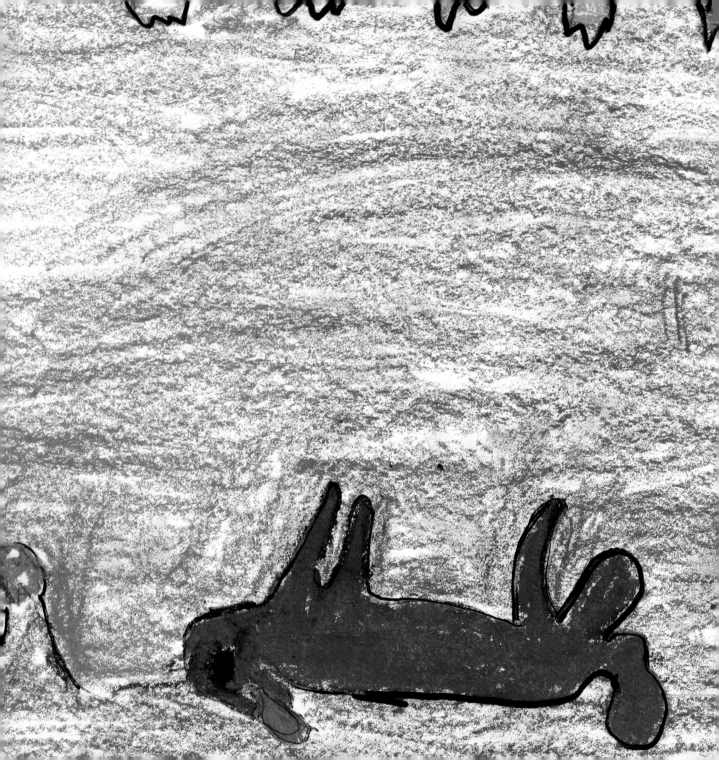

Iisaw a'ni/hin'ur pusùmtiqe, pay okiw,
pangso yukilti.

   Yan yaw Tsiròot Iisawuy hìntsatsna.

Coyote hit the ground hard, the poor thing,
and he met his end there.

   So this is how the Birds took care
of Coyote.

Pu'yaw Tsiròot pàngqaqwa,
"Yantani um'i. Naapas um itamuy
yuuyùynaniqey ankyangw itamumi atsata."

Then the Birds said to Coyote,
"This is the way you will have to be.
It's your own fault, since you wanted
to hurt us by lying to us."

Pay uma Iisawuy, okiw, u'nayani, hak oovi himu nen pay panwat naahàalayngwu.

So remember what happened to poor Coyote, and always be happy with yourself just the way you are.

Pay yuk pölö

The End

The Hopi Alphabet

An alphabet is a set of letters that is used to write a language. As we know, the English alphabet, **a** through **z**, has 26 letters. The Hopi alphabet has 21 letters.

The letters that are underlined in the following Hopi examples correspond to the sound of the letters that are underlined in the English examples in the right-hand column. Explanations are given in parentheses. Remember that explanations on paper can only approximate the true sounds of Hopi; it is always best to listen to a Hopi speaker to learn the proper pronunciations.

The pronunciations described below are based on the Third Mesa dialect; they can easily be adapted for use by Second and First Mesa speakers.

Let's begin by learning the Hopi vowels.

The Hopi Vowels

Vowels	As in the Hopi Word	Sounds like English
a	m*a*tsàakwa—horned toad	f*a*ther
e	p*e*hu—kangaroo rat	b*e*t
i	s*i*nom—people	h*ea*t
o	h*o*hoyaw—stink bug	h*o*le

ö	nöhu—egg	(while pronouncing the *a* in the English word "at," bring the lips together as if you were going to whistle, and round the sides of the tongue. This sound is made at the front of the mouth.)
u	t*u*va—nut	p*u*t

y is sometimes used as a vowel, as well as a consonant, just as in English:

y	ki'*y*ta—live	(pronounced like the *i*, but a little softer)

The Long and the Short of It

Hopi vowels can be short or long in their duration. The sound of the vowel is the same in either case, but the sound is drawn out nearly twice as long in long vowels.

Short vowels are written with a single letter; for example, the word *sinom*, "people," has a "short *i*," or just one *i* in its first syllable.

Long vowels are written with a double vowel; for example, *iisaw*, "coyote," has a "long *i*"; the *i* is doubled up, to draw out the sound in length.

The difference in vowel length in Hopi is important, as can be seen in these two words: *pep* (with a short *e*) means "at that point there," while *peep* (with a long *ee*) means "almost."

Some other examples of long vowels are

p*oo*ta—basket   *oo*maw—cloud

kan*ee*lo—sheep   p*aa*kiw—fish

w*uu*wanta—be thinking m*uu*yaw—moon

And some words have both long and
short vowels:

t*aa*w*a*—sun

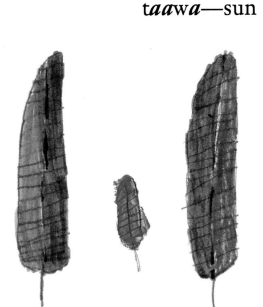

The Hopi Consonants

Now let's look at the consonants. For the most part the Hopi consonants are just like, or similar to, English consonants.

h	*H*opi—a Hopi person	*h*at
k	*K*atsina—Kachina	*k*ey
l	*l*eetayo—fox	*l*ove
m	*m*aana—girl	*m*an
n	*n*apna—shirt	*n*o
p	*p*oovoli—butterfly	*p*et

q	*q*aa'ö—corn	(pronounced like the English letter **k,** only farther back in the throat)
s	*s*owi—jackrabbit	*s*it
t	*t*ihu—doll	*t*all
v	ki*v*a—ceremonial room	*v*ery
w	*w*aakasi—cow	*w*alk
y	*y*ooyangw—rain	*y*ellow

73

Two Hopi _r_'s Are Better Than One

Hopi has two consonant sounds that are written like the English *r*, but pronounced very differently.

r <u>followed by a vowel</u> has a "zh" sound, something like the *s* in "measure," or the *z* in "azure." This *r* is called a voiced *r*, since it has a sound, or voice, to it.

r   *r*aana—frog   (somewhat like the *z* in "azure")

Another example of the voiced *r*:

r   *r*ookop—seventeen   (as if it were spelled *zh*ookop)

r <u>not followed</u> by a vowel sounds like "sh" but with the tongue curled up toward the roof of the mouth. This *r* is called an unvoiced *r*, since it has no voice, or sound, only a rush of air.

| *r* | ku*r*—perhaps | (rhymes with the English word "push," only with the tongue curled up) |

Another example of the unvoiced *r*:

| *r* | wa*r*ta—be a good runner | (pronounced "washta" but with the tongue curled up) |

The Last Stop . . .

is a consonant which is called the "stop," or a glottal stop in linguistic terms. It is written like this— ' , just like an English apostrophe.

We already know how to use a glottal stop from saying the English word "uh-oh;" you can see that in English we use the hyphen to represent the stopping of the voice. This catch in the voice between the two parts of the word is just like the Hopi "stop." Here is a simple Hopi example:

' a'a—piñon jay   uh-oh

Sometimes a word can have more than one stop:
yu'a'ata—to be talking

Consonant Clusters

Certain letters in Hopi are always pronounced together. The English letter **g** is part of the Hopi language, but it is only used with **n**. With **n**, it forms the following consonant clusters:

ng   **ngw**   **ngy**

The **ng** combination sounds just like the nasal **ng** in the English word "song." In this example it is placed at the beginning of the word:

ng   **nga**hu—medicine

In order to pronounce the other **ng** combinations, just say "ng" and add on the sound of a **w**, or a **y**.

ngw   niikya**ngw**—but
ngy   **ngy**aw—meow (a cat's cry)

The **ng**, **ngw**, and **ngy** clusters are used frequently.

Other combinations that are pronounced together, except in rare cases, are **kw, ky,** and **ts.**

kw	**kw**aahu—eagle	(like the **qu** in **qu**een)
ky	**ky**aaro—parrot	(like the **k** in s**k**ewer)
ts	**ts**iro—bird	(like the **ts** in ca**ts**)

And Finally . . .

Hopi language is creative. Sounds are often used playfully, especially in songs, for artistic effect:

Poota, poota, poooota,
Poota, poota, poooota,
Yowa ini, yowa ini,
Phhu, phhu, phhu.

Hopi to English Glossary

The following is a list of words that occur in this story. They are given meanings for the story here, but may have different meanings in other stories or general conversation. Some nouns are listed in their objective form, meaning that they are used in the sentence as an object, just as some nouns are used in English sentences as objects.

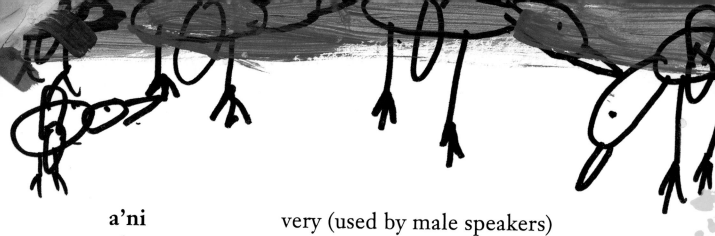

a'ni	very (used by male speakers)
ahoy	back to
akw	by means of, with
amumi	toward them
amumum	with them
angqw	from
ankyangw	with the thought of
as	like to
atkyamiq	toward a point way down below
atsata	to lie, tell falsehoods
aw	into it, toward it
ayo'	out of the way, away
engem	for, for the benefit of
ep	at, in, on
hak	someone, one
himu	something
hin	somehow

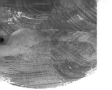

hin'ur	very (used by female speakers)
hìntsaknuma	be going around doing something
hìntsatsna	do something to, take care of
Iisaw	Coyote
Iisawuy	Coyote (objective case)
ini	things in a basket
ìntotat	after putting things in a basket
it	this (objective case)
itàamasay	our own feathers
itam	we
itamumi	to us, toward us
itamuy	us (objective case)
ki'yyungwa	were living, residing
kita	says, said
kwangwawuwanta	scheming, having pleasurable thoughts
maqayani	will give
masa'yta	have wings, have feathers
masay	their own feathers
na'uyi'ykyangw	while hiding
naahàalayngwu	be happy with one's self
naapas	one's own fault
nàmtötötima	to tumble down through the air

nen	and so, accordingly
ngu'ani	will catch, will nab
niikyangw	but
niqw	and, when
nu'	I
okiw	poor thing
oomiq	to go up high
oova	up high
oovi	that's why
Orayve	at Oraibi
pàasat	then, at that time
pam	he, she, it
pàngqaqwa	they said, they spoke to
pàngqawu	he, she, it said
pangso	there, at that place
pantsatskyaqw	while doing something
panwat	in that way
pasìwnaya	they planned
pay	so, now
phhu	(sound made when blowing the chaff away from the seed during winnowing)
pitu	arrives, arrived

piw	also, again
pölö	ending
pongitotangwu	they would be picking
poooota	(same as *poota*, winnowing basket)
poota	winnowing basket
pootat	winnowing basket (objective case)
pooyantotangwu	they would be blowing, blow away the chaff
posto	be falling down
postokyangw	and be falling down even further
pu'	then
puma	they
pusùmtiqe	when he hit the ground with a thud
puuyàltini	will fly
puuyàltoti	they flew up
puuyàltotikyàakyangw	as they flew upward
puuyàltotiqw	when they flew up
puuyawma	he was flying along

qa	not
sen	perhaps
sivosit	grass seeds (objective case)
sùukyawa	one of them
taa!	now!
taavang	southwest
tawlalwakyàakyangw	while they were singing
tawlalwangwu	usually singing
taytaqe	as he was watching
tömö'iwmaqw	since winter was coming
töqti	called out, shouted
töqtotingwu	they would call out
tsaayankyàakyangw	as they winnowed
tsaayantotaqam	those who are winnowing
tsaayantotaqe	because they were winnowing
tsìipuyat	its chaff (objective case)
tsii riw riw riw	(playful cry of the Birds, from *tsiro*, "birds")
Tsiro	Bird
Tsiròot	Birds
Tsiròotuy	Birds (objective case)

tsöngmokiwta	to be hungry
tsotspitota	they snatched, pulled out
tumala'yyungwa	they were working
tutwa	see, notice
Tuuwanasavit	the place called Tuuwanasavi (objective case)
um	you
um'i	you're the one
umumum	with all of you
u'nayani	will remember
ung	you (objective case)
wuuwanta	be thinking
ya	(indicates a question)
yan	this way
yantani	will be this way
yaw	it is said

yeesiwa	they were living
yeeva!	smack! (hit against by falling)
yep	here
yowa	(a nonsense word; derivation unknown)
yuk	here, to this point
yukilti	to come to an end, be done with
yuuyuynaniqey	mistreat someone, hurt someone
yuwsinaya	they dressed up (Coyote)

English to Hopi Glossary

Hopi, like all languages, is "context-sensitive." Words take on meanings or shades of meaning based on how they are used. This English/Hopi glossary is included here to help with cross-referencing.

after putting things in a basket	ìntotat
also, again	piw
and, when	niqw
and so, accordingly	nen
arrives, arrived	pitu
as he was watching	taytaqe

as they flew upward	puuyàltotikyàakyangw
as it was falling	postokyangw
as they winnowed	tsaayankyàakyangw
at Oraibi	Orayve
at, in, on	ep
back to	ahoy
because they were winnowing	tsaayantotaqe
be going around doing something	hìntsaknuma
be falling down	posto
be happy with one's self	naahàalayngwu
be thinking	wuuwanta
Bird	Tsiro
Birds	Tsiròot
Birds (objective case)	Tsiròotuy

Birds' playful cry	tsii riw riw riw
from *tsiro*, "birds")	
but	niikyangw
by means of, with	akw
called out, shouted	töqti
(its) chaff (objective case)	tsìipuyat
Coyote	Iisaw
Coyote (objective case)	Iisawuy
do something to,	hìntsatsna
take care of	
ending	pölö
for, for the benefit of	engem
from	angqw
grass seeds (objective case)	sivosit
have wings, have feathers	masa'yta
he was flying	puuyawma

he, she, it	pam
he, she, it said	pàngqawu
here	yep
here, to this point	yuk
I	nu'
in that way	panwat
(indicates a question)	ya
into it, toward it	aw
it is said	yaw
like to	as
mistreat someone, hurt someone	yuuyuynaniqey
(nonsense word; derivation unknown)	yowa
not	qa
now!	taa!
one of them	sùukyawa
one's own fault	naapas
our own feathers	itàamasay
out of the way, away	ayo'
perhaps	sen
poor thing	okiw

says, said	kita
scheming, having pleasurable thoughts	kwangwawuwanta
see, notice	tutwa
since winter was coming	tömö'iwmaqw
smack! (sound of something hitting the ground)	yeeva!
so, now	pay
somehow	hin
someone, one	hak
something	himu
(sound made when blowing chaff away)	phhu
southwest	taavang
that's why	oovi
the place called Tuuwanasavi (objective case)	Tuuwanasavit
their own feathers	masay
then	pu'
then, at that time	pàasat
there, at that place	pangso

they	puma
they dressed him up	yuwsinaya
they flew up	puuyàltoti
they planned	pasìwnaya
they said, they spoke to	pàngqaqwa
they snatched, pulled out	tsotspitota
they were living	yeesiwa
they were working	tumala'yyungwa
they winnowed	tsaayankyàakyangw
they would be picking	pongitotangwu
they would call out	töqtotingwu
they would winnow, blow away the chaff	pooyantotangwu
things in a basket	ini
this (objective case)	it
this way	yan

those who are winnowing	tsaayantotaqam
to be hungry	tsöngmokiwta
to come to an end, be done with	yukilti
to go up high	oomiq
to lie, tell falsehoods	atsata
to tumble down through the air	nàmtötötima
to us, toward us	itamumi
toward a point way down below	atkyamiq
toward them	amumi
up high	oova
us (objective case)	itamuy
usually singing	tawlalwangwu
very (used by female speakers)	hin'ur
very (used by male speakers)	a'ni
we	itam
were living, residing	ky'yyungwa
when he hit the ground	pusùmtiqe
when they flew up	puuyàltotiqw

while doing something	pantsatskyaqw
while hiding	na'uyi'ykyangw
while they were singing	tawlalwakyàakyangw
will be this way	yantani
will catch, will nab	ngu'ani
will fly	puuyàltini
will give	maqayani
will remember	u'nayani
winnowing basket	poota
winnowing basket (objective case)	pootat
with all of you	umumum
with the thought of	ankyangw
with them	amumum
you	um
you (objective case)	ung
you're the one	um'i